Castle
La Corona
de los Santos

Cook Book

With 25 Authentic Costa Rican Recipes

by
James Nathaniel Holland

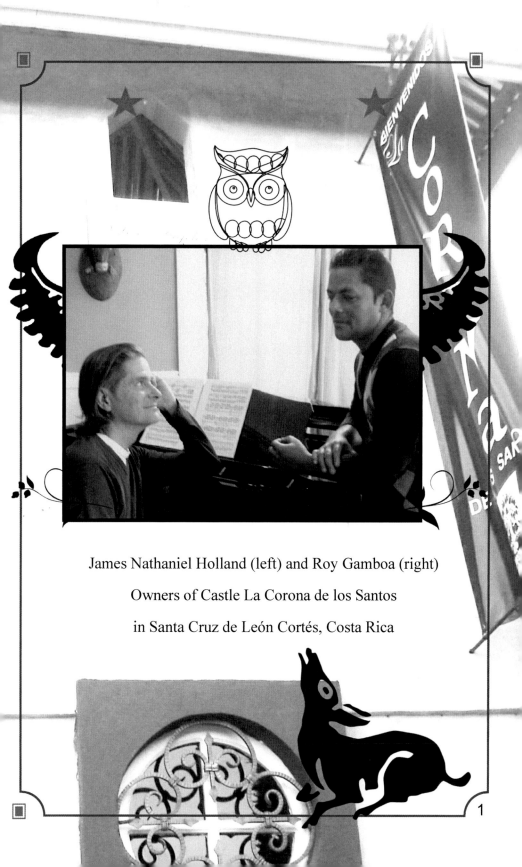

James Nathaniel Holland (left) and Roy Gamboa (right)

Owners of Castle La Corona de los Santos

in Santa Cruz de León Cortés, Costa Rica

Yet another rainbow at Castle La Corona de los Santos.

Photo: Roy Gamboa

¡Bienvenidos!

"It has been widely known for years that these mountains hold secrets," a sentence that had escaped from the lips of a senile centenarian of the town, "secrets that are better kept that way, secret."*

Fortunately for us, the recipes of this enchanted valley in Costa Rica, known as "Los Santos" are not.

Contained in these pages are authentic mountain dishes, and many of my favorites, that I use to delight our guests.

Fresh fruits and vegetables of the mountains are almost always readily available and the only challenge of cooking these dishes is to let the natural flavor come forth without adding a lot of unnecessary extras.

Come vist us at Castle La Corona de los Santos to try them first hand, or enjoy making them in your own home!

As they say in Costa Rica . . .

¡Buen Provecho!

James Nathaniel Holland

All Original Photos by: Roy Gamboa and James N Holland

* From the book, "Legends and Other Fantastic and Strange Tales from Castle La Corona de Los Santos"

Spanish Lesson

¡Buen Provecho! – 'Bon appetite!'

Buen Cuchara – referring to the delicious creations of a talented cook

Carne – generally meat, more specifically, beef

Casero – home-made

Dulce – a type of pure, raw sugar boiled from cane juice. Sold in cakes. Can substitute brown sugar, but not the same.

Picadillo – a type of salad that usually include a some kind of starch, like cooked potatoes, bits of meat, cilantro and vegetables. It is usually eaten with tortillas.

Tortillas – a very then, flat patty made from white or yellow cornmeal, a TB of shortening, 1 tsp. salt, and water to desired consistency and cook on a hot, flat surface. Usually need a tortilla press. Takes some experience to make them well.

Gallo – similar to a *picadillo*, an appetizer.

Leche – milk

Queso – cheese

Arroz – rice

Natilla – a cross between yogurt and sour cream, not really one or the other, usually made at home. You may substitute sour cream.

Queso Turrialba – A semi-soft cheese that one can fry, named after the Turrialba volcano. Try substituting semi-soft ricotta cheese

¡Qué Rico! – 'How tasty.' *"Jrjjjico!" (in Costa Rica)* - Incredibly good!

¡Juééé?! – 'You go on!' or in England equivalent to "rather!"

Masa Flour – white corn flour, should not be confused with yellow corn meal

Nicaragua

Costa Rica

Caribbean Sea

Panama

Pacific Ocean

Castle La Corona
de los Santos

The mountains of Santa Cruz de León Cortés, Costa Rica

Photo: James N. Holland

Some Common
Cultivars of the Mountains

| Coffee "Cafe" | Passionfruit "Grenadilla" | Avocado "Aguacate" |

Peruvian Guava
"Guayabita"

All Varieties of
Oranges and Lemons

Medlar
"Nispero"

Costa Rican Guava
"Cas"

Peach
"Durazno"

Narajilla

Other Fruits: Apples, Raspberries ("Mora")

Some Common
Cultivars of the Mountains

Fava Beans
"Cubasas"

Vegetable Pears
"Chayotes"

Zucchini
"Zapallo"

Pumpkin
"Ayote"

Rosemary
"Romero"

Calendula

Fennel
"Hinojo"

Hibiscus
"Clavelón"

And Many More!

A sunflower raises its head to the warm sun.

Photo: Roy Gamboa

Appetizers And Dips

Locally grown avocados in Santa Cruz de León Cortés, Costa Rica

Photo: Roy Gamboa

Dips and Gallos

Chimichurri (or Pico de Gallo)

(Serves 2)

2 fresh large tomatoes: 1 peeled, 1 with skin
1 large sweet red bell pepper
1 hot Capsaicin pepper *(opt.)*
1 large Spanish onion
1 tsp salt   **4 TB apple cider vinegar**

By hand, cube all vegetables. If using a food processor, only lightly chop the onion and bell peppers separately and combine later. Cube the tomatoes by hand. Finely chop herbs, and combine all in a stainless steel bowl. Add salt, sugar, oil, vinegar, etc. to the mixture. Subtly adjust to preferred taste, maintaining the ratio of salt to sugar to vinegar.

Refried Beans (or Bean Dip)

(Beans, see p. 29)

Guacamole

(Serves 4)

3 just ripe, Haas avocados
1 large sweet bell pepper
1 small Spanish onion
1 small clove of garlic, minced
1 medium tomato, unpeeled
1 tsp salt
¼ tsp of chili powder *(or powdered ground cumin and paprika)*

Using a food processor, blender, or by hand, chop as finely as you can the onion, bell pepper, cilantro, spices and garlic. Peel avocados by scoring a complete ring around it, take out seeds, and scoop out the meat with a large spoon. If this the avocado is not soft enough to do this, It is not ripe yet, and use another.

Mix in ½ of the required avocados. Use the machine to make a somewhat smooth mixture. Chop the rest of the avocados into medium pieces. Then roughly mix these in.

Accompany any or all above with fresh with fried tortillas chips (p. 12)
or green plantains (p. 13)

eep ried

Why pay an expensive price for the bagged tortilla chips, when you can use this simple recipe. They taste better and you also control the `amount of salt used.

Home-made Tortilla Chips
(Serves 2)

6 medium-sized, fresh, Tortillas (Corn or Flour)
1 deep fryer or an old pot filled with sunflower oil (about 3 cm)
Salt
Lime (if desired)

Quarter the tortillas and create triangular wedges. Heat oil and when hot, put wedges into the oil. Turn the heat on about level 5. Do not cook at too high of heat. Watch for desired brownness. They can sometimes cook very fast.

Remove from oil with tongs and place on a plate with a paper towel to absorb excess oil. Sprinkle lightly with salt and juice from a lime wedge.

Eat with our recipes for Dips or *Gallos* from the previous page.

Fried Yuca
(Serves 3)

1 medium sized Yuca Root
1 pot of water
1 deep fryer or an old pot filled with sunflower oil (about 3 cm)
Salt

Yuca (or Cassava, Manioc) is poisonous when eaten raw, so cut off both ends of the yuca root and thoroughly peel it. If large, cut it in half and then slice into large "french fry" shaped pieces.

When buying the yuca, break it open and make sure it is white in color and doesn't have black or grayish streaks running through the inside.

Bring a medium-sized pot of water to a vigorous boil. Place the sliced yuca pieces in the pot and boil at medium heat until completely tender.

Next, heat up deep fryer or small, old (but clean) pot of your oil. Fry until golden brown. Take out place on a paper towel and salt as desired.

Plantains

Plantains deserve their own page. The only difference between the salty ("Patacones," because it looks like somebody stepped on it) or the sweet ("Maduros") you may get in the restaurant is the amount of time it has been given to ripen.

Plantains (Salty) "Patacones"

1 Green, Unripe Plantain
Something to use as a press
1 deep fryer or an old pot
filled with sunflower oil
(about 3 cm)
Salt to taste
A squeeze of lime *(opt.)*

Peel the plantain by scoring it long ways with a knife. Place it under cold, running water and peel it back with your fingers.

Slice the peeled plantain long ways and somewhat thick. Heat up your oil. Place in oil and fry for about 5 or so minutes. Remove from oil with tongs and flatten them with either a tortilla press or two small cutting boards, etc. Be creative!

Put flattened pieces back into the fryer with enough space that they float. Let fry until golden brown. Take out and place on a plate covered with a paper towel.

Sprinkle with salt and eat with ketchup. Great with guacamole!

Plantains (Sweet) "Maduros"

1 ripe, yellow Plantain
1 skillet with sunflower oil
(about 3 cm)

For sweet plantains, again peel the plantain by scoring it long ways with a knife. This time it should be easy to remove the peel without any water.

Thinly slice the peeled plantain long ways. Heat up your skillet. Place in and fry until browning begins.

Be sure to watch them carefully because after a certain point, they will begin to burn.

Serve as is or add a small clove of minced garlic cilantro leaves.

Or try them warm with shreds of Monterey Jack cheese

Architectural detail at Castle La Corona de los Santos, Costa Rica

Photo: James N Holland

Soups

La Corona de los Santos Chili

(Serves 6, Can be stored in refrigerator)

1 large iron skillet
1 large sauce pot

2 cups of red kidney beans
4 large ripe red tomatoes
1/2 lb. of fresh ground beef
1 large onion
1 large red bell pepper
1 large Spanish onion
1 Scotch bonnet hot pepper (whole)
2 medium cloves of garlic, minced

1 tsp Fresh cilantro
1TB Fresh Spring onions
1 sprig Fresh thyme
1 leaf Fresh basil
1 tsp Fresh oregano
1 tsp Rosemary

1 tsp salt
2 TB of brown sugar (or "dulce" raw sugar)
2 TB Chili powder
3 TB olive oil
1/2 tsp black pepper

(Opt. 3 leaves Fresh wormwood (or "anjejo" in Spanish) Pictured above.)

Using a food processor, or by hand, roughly chop the vegetables, somewhat fine, but not too much. Separately, finely chop the herbs and set aside. Liquidate the tomatoes.

Cook on high the kidney beans with plenty of water in a crock pot until tender. Do not add salt because salt will inhibit the absorption of the water into the beans.

In the skillet brown the ground beef. Pour the beans with its juice into your sauce pot. Put in all ingredients, except the herbs. Simmer the lowest heat your stove will go for about 20 minutes. Around the last 5 minutes, add the herbs and before serving sprinkle fresh herbs on top. Serve alone or on top of white rice.

Basic Tomato Sauce or Soup

(Serves 6)

1 large sauce pot or iron skillet
4 peeled large ripe tomato
1/4 cup of fresh ground beef (opt.)
1 medium Spanish onion
1 red bell pepper
1 medium clove of garlic, minced
1 tsp Parsley
1 sprig Fresh thyme
1 leaf Fresh basil
1 tsp Fresh Greek oregano
1 tsp of rosemary
1 tsp salt
3 TB olive oil
1/2 tsp black pepper

Using a food processor, or by hand, roughly chop the vegetables, somewhat fine, but not too much. Separately, finely chop the herbs and set aside.

Liquidate tomatoes.

Brown ground beef, put in vegetables except the tomatoes. Cook on low until tender. Add tomatoes puree. Simmer for about 30 min. Add herbs.

Serve over meat or your favorite pasta.

Camote	Yuca	Tiquisque	Green
(Sweet	(Cassava,		Plantain
Potato)	Manioc)		

Root Stew (Rondon) with optional Fish

(Serves 6, Can be stored in refrigerator and eaten cold)

1 large sauce pan
1 wooden, stirring spoon

4 fillets of corvina (sea bass) of talapia *(opt.)*
1/2 cup of milk
1 TB of unsalted butter
1/4 cup of dry, white sherry (optional)

1 large onion
1 stalk of celery with leaves
1 tsp. of salt
Black and White Pepper to taste

1 medium camote (see above)
1 medium tiquisque (see above)
1/2 of large yuca root
1 medium peeled carrot
1 medium peeled potato
1 large green plantain *(i.e., not ripe)*

1 medium clove of garlic, minced
1 tsp Fresh cilantro
1 tsp. of Fresh fennel
1 sprig Fresh thyme
1 chopped or (snipped with scissors) leaf of leek
1 tsp chives

From the Caribbean!

First peel and chop all the root vegetables into bite-sized chunks. Then put potatoes, carrots, yucca, plantains in the saucepan and cover with water. Boil until tender, then add the camote and tiquisque until tender.

Now use the water from this, turn down stove to low as it will go and add the rest of the ingredients and cover, stirring occasionally. If stove has really low heat, like an electric stove, simmer for about 30 minutes. With gas around 20. The lower you can keep the heat the more the flavors will rise. As always after you add the herbs, be careful not to over-cook. And fish in general rarely takes long to cook.

Serve hot or try cold in nice bowls to guests. Compliment with white French bread.

Fava Bean (Cubasas) Soup

(Serves 4)

2 cups of cooked (soft) red or fava beans	Sprigs of Thyme
2 cups of cold water or bean	1 tsp Oregano
liquid leftover from cooking the beans	1 tsp Fennel
1 red or green sweet pepper	1 tsp chives
1 hot pepper	4 sprigs of cilantro
1 small Spanish onion	
1 medium clove of garlic, minced	
1 tsp coffee grounds	

1 TB olive oil
1 tsp brown sugar *(or dulce "raw sugar")*
1 TB Dry Sherry *(optional)*
1 tsp Salt, and pepper to taste
  (opt. ¼ kg. of pork butt *(or poste de cerdo)* **finely chopped)**

Chop well the sweet peppers and onions and sauté in a medium saucepan with the garlic in the olive oil until almost soft. Add beans, water and all the other ingredients, except the herbs. Bring to a quick boil and immediately turn down on low. Finely snip the herbs with scissors into the soup. Simmer on low for about 15 min, not letting it boil too much.

Peach Palm ("Pejibaye") Soup

(Serves 4)

6 or 7 pejibayes

1 small can of sweet corn or one cob, cooked

2 chives
1 large onion
1 large red sweet pepper
1 tablespoon vegetable shortening
1 tablespoon mayonnaise
1 tablespoon sour cream *(or 'natilla')*
1 cup milk
¼ cup of Slivered almonds or Pine Nuts
Salt and Pepper to Taste

Boil the pejibayes very, very well. Run cold water over them to cool, and place on a cutting board. Slice the tops off, place upside down and peel off the skin. Slice the sides to the seed and take seeds out. If you like just eat them like this with mayonnaise and salt as an appetizer.

In a blender, add pejibayes, spread, herbs, onion, corn, and chicken, if using it, with the cup of milk to puree. Pour out in a medium pot. Set to medium low heat. Salt and pepper to taste. Let cook for about 20 min more, stirring every once in a while, making sure that the soup does not bubble too much or burn. When ready serve in bowls and sprinkle almonds or pine nuts on top. Serve hot or try cold with toasted cheese sandwiches.

Note: Never use garlic with pejibayes, for it will ruin the taste of them for you.

Castle La Corona de los Santos, Costa Rica
above the Labyrinth Garden

Photo: Roy Gamboa

The Sapphire Room at
Castle La Corona de los Santos, Costa Rica

Photo: James N Holland

Meals And Meats

Eggs

Scrambled Eggs, a La Corona

(Serves 4)

8 eggs
2 TB heavy cream *(or natilla)*
Dash of Soy Sauce
1 tsp salt
1 leak, chopped
1 small onion, chopped
2 TB Olive oil
Pepper

First of all, **never, ever** be tempted to use garlic or parsley with eggs, unless you like the taste of "wet•dog." Using cream, yogurt, sour cream, or *natilla* will guarantee a fluffy consistency.

Put oil in a skillet and heat to only low-medium heat. Crack open eggs and put into a bowl, add soy sauce, cream, and salt Next, pour into heated skillet and stir them vigorously. Add extras now, except any herbs or spices. Use spatula to skim the bottom of the skillet as eggs firm. Keep doing this until eggs are almost all cooked. Add herbs, sprinkle with paprika before serving.

Huevos Rancheros (Poached Eggs)

(Serves 4)

This recipe is actually a combination of "Refried Beans" (p. 29), Pico de Gallo (p. 11), Tortilla Chips (p. 12) and the Poached eggs, below.)

8 eggs
2 TB Olive oil
2 TB White Vinegar
Salt
Pepper
Paprika

Put out eggs and let them set to room temperature for at least 30 minutes.

Put the oil in a deep skillet and fill it with water, vinegar, and oil. Bring it to a vigorous boil. For each egg, take a small glass cup and ever so gently crack open the egg, not breaking the yoke. Take the glass cup, with the edge touching the top of the boiling water, and let the egg slide out of the cup into the water. Repeat for each of the eggs. Take a slotted flat spoon, and when eggs are cooked, about 3 min. Scoop them, let them drain, and place them on the serving dish. Sprinkle with fresh herbs, salt, pepper, and/or paprika.

Fajitas (Beef, Chicken or Pork)

(Serves 4)

**1 whole chicken breast without bone, or
1 medium sirloin steak (without bone),
or pork chop**

**1 tsp of soy sauce
1 TB of olive oil
1 small red or green sweet pepper,
thinly sliced
1 small Spanish onion, thinly sliced
1 medium clove of garlic, minced
1 TB Sugar** *(or dulce or brown sugar)*

**Pinch of Salt and Pepper
Leaves from a sprig of Thyme
3 oregano leaves,
finely chopped
1 tsp of chopped chives,
finely chopped
1 tsp of chopped cilantro**

Many times you can find the meat already sliced for you. Slice meat of choice into strips. On a hot griddle sauté the meat in olive oil and put on the soy sauce and sugar. It is done when excess water nearly all evaporates. Set aside. Now sauté the vegetables with salt and pepper and herbs until vegetables are soft. Mix vegetables with the meat. Serve and eat with tortillas, either corn or flour.

Chicharones (Fried Pork)

(Serves 5)

**1 Deep Fryer or iron pot over open fire
1 kilogram of pork butt (poste)
3 medium cloves Garlic, minced
3 TB of Sugar** *(or dulce)*
1 tsp. salt

**Soy Sauce
2 TB of dry white wine or
apple cider vinegar
1 TB Corn Starch
½ Half fresh lime**

Cut the pork into chunks about 2 cm x 2 cm. Boil pork until cooked with the garlic, sugar, soy sauce, and wine. Be careful to not overcook. When ready, take out of the water and roll them in the corn starch. Deep fry in oil until almost brown. Take out and put on a paper towel. They will continue to brown a little bit. Sprinkle salt to taste and squeeze lime juice over them. Serve with ketchup and mayonnaise and lime wedges. Try combination of cooked *fava* beans, fresh avocado and Pico de Gallo.

Tuna and Pasta

(Serves 4)

1 ½ cup dried pasta *(penne or zitti)*
1 can of tuna, packed in water

**1 TB of soy sauce
1 TB of olive oil
1 small red or green sweet pepper,
thinly sliced
1 small Spanish onion, thinly sliced
1 medium carrot, thinly sliced
1 medium tomato, wedged
1/3 cup of black olives, sliced
1 medium clove of garlic, minced**

**Pinch of Salt and Pepper
Leaves from a sprig of Thyme
3 oregano leaves,
finely chopped
1 tsp of chopped chives,
finely chopped
1 tsp of chopped rosemary**

In a medium sauce pan, prepare dried pasta as directed on the package. Separately, open the can of tuna and drain. Once again separately, in a large iron skillet, sauté the carrots and garlic in olive oil for about 2 minutes. Next add the peppers and onions. Turn heat on low. Toss in with a spatula, the cooked pasta, the black olives and tuna. Add spices and herbs and soy sauce. Turn off skillet and let set for 5 minutes before serving.

Pork Chops (Chuletas)

(Serves 4)

4   medium pork chops
2   TB of olive oil
3   TB of fresh Sage, chopped
Salt and pepper

In an iron skillet, sauté the pork chops in the olive oil on medium heat. Add salt and pepper. When thoroughly cooked, add the fresh sage. Toss and serve.

Carne a la Parilla *(Pictured on page 21)*

(Serves 4)

4 medium steaks, or 2 whole chicken breasts with bone cut in half
A grill 30 cm above an open fire, wood of cypress or eucalyptus,
   chopped about 25 cm x 5 cm
5 TB of fresh Rosemary, torn with fingers
Lime
1/3 cup salt / Pepper to taste / *(Opt. paprika and turmeric)*

Prepare your fire and it is important to let it almost burn down until the wood is white. Meanwhile, rub the meat liberally with the salt and spices. Under the skin (if chicken), place the rosemary. It is important to let the meat warm up to room temperature. Place on grill and try not to move it (about 20 min.). Maintain heat by adding more wood, but not too much. Turn over and grill until inside is cooked. Squeeze the lime over the meat before serving.

Olla de Carne

(Serves 10)

Believe it or not, slow cooking in a slow cooker or "Olla" is very Costa Rican. The meat falls apart like butter and the flavors retain much more of their taste.

1   kilogram of stew beef or pork *(trocitos)*
2   sweet corn cobs divided into 3 cm pieces
2   large potatoes, quartered and peeled
1   large carrot divided into 3 pieces
1   medium yuca, peeled and cut into large chunks
1   green plantain, peeled and cut into large chunks
1   large onion, cut into chunks and peeled
1   clove of garlic, whole
1   tsp of Salt
½ tsp pepper

Fresh Herbs of:
Thyme
Oregano
Rosemary
Parsley

Place all ingredients in slow cooker and just cover with water. Turn it on to low heat and let cook for 8 hours or more.

When finished, all into a saucepan and allow to "rest" before serving. Serve with hot sauce or *Tobasco*.

Cheesy

Castilian Toasted Cheese Sandwiches

(Makes 1)

2   slices of Integral pre-sliced bread
1   tsp of vegetable spread
1   tsp mayonnaise *(optional)*

1   tsp of olive oil
1   small **red** or green sweet pepper, thinly sliced
1   small **Spanish** onion, thinly sliced
1   medium clove of garlic, minced

Slice a ½ of your favorite cheese, *Terrano*,
cheddar, mozzarella, edam, etc.

Pinch of Salt
Pepper
Leaves from a sprig of Thyme
3   oregano leaves, finely chopped
1   tsp of chopped chives, finely chopped

On a hot griddle sauté the vegetables with salt and pepper and herbs until vegetables are soft. Butter one side of both slices of bread. Place buttered side on the griddle. On the other side of one slice, spread mayo and layer the vegetables, the cheese and the herbs. T op with the other slice, buttered side up on top. Watch until golden brown, flip and brown other side. Eat whole or cut sandwich diagonally.

Quesedillas

(Makes 12 triangular quarters)

6 medium flour tortillas
1 tsp of olive oil
1 small red or green sweet
  pepper,thinly sliced
1 small Spanish onion, thinly sliced
1 medium clove of garlic, minced

Pinch of Salt and Pepper
Leaves from a sprig of Thyme
3 oregano leaves,
  finely chopped
1 tsp of chopped chives,
  finely chopped
1 tsp of chopped cilantro

On a hot griddle sauté the vegetables with salt and pepper and herbs until vegetables are soft. Place 3 of the tortillas on the griddle, layer equally the vegetable mixture and the cheese. Top the each of the 3 tortillas with other 3, making 3 sandwiches. Watch until beginning to harden and brown, flip and brown other side. Cut each *quesadilla* in triangular quarters.

Tortillas con Queso

How they taste so good on a cold day or as a side for breakfast! '¡Qué Rico!'

1   cup masa corn meal (white or yellow corn)
1   cup milk
1   tsp unsalted butter or vegetable shortening
1   tsp salt
2   TB of sour cream *(or natilla)*
Pepper to taste
1/3 cup of mozzarella or jack cheese (Terrano or Monte Rico)**,**
finely chopped
Skillet or griddle
Corn oil
A sheet of wax paper

Heat the oil in the skillet as hot as can be without burning the oil. Do not use olive oil, because olive oil has a low burning point.

In a medium mixing bowl, put the 1 cup of yellow corn meal, salt, and pepper. Cut the unsalted butter into small pieces and mix in with your fingers until it resembles coarse crumbs (or use pastry blender).

Slowly add the milk, mixing well with a fork until mixture becomes doughy. Mix in the sour cream. Let rest for 10 min. Mix in the cheese. Knead well.

Roll the dough into about the size of a tennis ball, then place on the griddle. Use the sheet of wax paper to flatten out the ball in the shape of a pancake. Fix any broken edges with your finger.

Cook until bottom is brown (see photo above) then flip over with a spatula and brown other side. Serve with a dollop of sour cream, fried egg on top, or with fried ham.

For dinner serve with stewed chicken in the tomato sauce recipe on page 16.

Sides

A magical stairwell that leads to the rooms at Castle La Corona

Photo: James N Holland

Beans

When Preparing Beans from Dried

There are no short cuts to preparing delicious beans from dried ones. You will need to use the slow cooker. For any dried bean, do not add salt before cooking. This will inhibit their absorption of water. Use about ¼ cup dried beans to every ¾ cups water.

Black beans will cook faster than the other types, so turn the crock pot on high first for about 15 minutes, then let cook about 3 hours on low or until beans are tender.

Red beans (Kidney Beans) are a different matter and take much longer. It is best to just put the crock pot on high and let them cook for about 4 to 5 hours until tender. Drain and store refrigerated, unsalted.

White beans prepare the same as black beans.

Refried Beans (Dip)

(Serves 4)

*Delicious and healthy, these go good
as a side with rice or tortilla chip dip
(see page 12.)*

**1 cup of cooked (soft) red beans
1 red or green sweet pepper
1 small Spanish onion
1 medium cloves of garlic, minced
¼ tsp. ground cumin
1 tsp coffee grounds
1 tsp Dulce or brown sugar
1 tsp. Salt / Pepper to taste**
(opt. 1 pork chop finely chopped)

Throw everything into a blender or food processor and add a tablespoon of water until you have a smooth paste. If you've added too much water just empty contents from the blender and pour into a skillet. Put it over low heat and add a little bit of flour, stir until it reaches the consistency you want.

T op with shredded mozzarella or Monterrey jack cheese and chopped leaves of cilantro. Spice up with chopped *jalapeño* peppers.

Fava Bean (Cubasa) Soup

(See page 18)

Rice

If Preparing Rice from Dried

Follow these directions for perfect rice every time: Use the ratio of 1 quantity of rice to every 1 ½ quantities of water. In the saucepan with rice and water, put a whole medium clove of garlic, 2 TB of oil and 1 tsp. of salt. Bring to a boil, turn down heat to 4 and let simmer for exactly 15 minutes.

If you want the rice to absorb more of the flavor of these recipes, just leave a little undercooked. For "sofrijo" add to the mixture before cooking, onion, bell pepper and carrots.

Gallo Pinto

(Serves 6, can be stored in refrigerator)

1 cup white rice
1 cup of black or red beans
(cooked) or drained from a can (adjust salt)
1 stalk celery
1/2 large carrot
1 large Spanish onion
1 large red bell pepper
1 clove of garlic, minced
1 tsp fresh cilantro
1 sprig fresh thyme
4 sprigs of fresh rosemary
1 tsp fresh Greek oregano
1 tsp salt
2 TB *dulce*
1 tsp. ground coffee
2 TB olive oil
1/4 tsp black pepper
Hot peppers *(opt.)* to taste
Salsa Inglesa to taste (a bottled sauce made in Costa Rica)
Soy Sauce

The National Dish of Costa Rica!

Using a food processor or by hand, chop vegetables fairly fine. Separately, finely chop the herbs and set aside. Add vegetables to rice and 1 ½ cups water in a medium sauce pan. Bring to a boil and let simmer for 14 minutes. Heat a large iron skillet to medium low. Combine the cooked beans, *dulce*, coffee, oil, and garlic (and hot peppers)

in the skillet. Let skillet mixture simmer for 5 min. covered. When rice/vegetables are ready, add to the beans mixture in the skillet and mix. Add salt, black pepper, sauces to taste. Stir. Lastly add herbs. Stir, cover and let simmer on low for about 15 min. Serve with fried eggs and a dab of *natilla* (sour cream). Dress with cilantro.

The national dish of Costa Rica, Gallo Pinto

Photo: James N Holland

Spanish Rice

I don't know exactly where this recipe came from, but I sure remember it on hot summer Saturday nights. Italian restaurants sometimes call it rissotto a la Roma Antigua. Whatever its origins, this dish is relatively healthy and very satisfying. You can substitute the risotto for the rice, but be sure to tweak it so that the risotto is cooked properly before combining.

(Serves 6, can be stored in refrigerator)

1 large iron skillet
3/4 cups white rice a little underdone
4 large peeled, ripe tomatoes
1/2 lb. of fresh ground beef
1 large onion
1 large red bell pepper
1 8 oz. can of sweet corn
1 large onion
2 medium cloves of garlic, minced
1 tsp Fresh cilantro
1/2 tsp. Fresh rosemary
1 sprig Fresh thyme
4 leaves fresh basil
1 tsp Fresh oregano

3 leaves fresh wormwood (or *"ajenjo mayor" in Spanish) (opt.)*
4 Panamanian hot peppers, or 2 garden hot peppers *(opt.)*
1 tsp salt
1 TB chile powder *(or combination of paprika, cumin, powdered onion)*
4 TB olive oil
1/4 tsp black pepper
Sprinkle of Paprika
2   slices of Monterey Jack Cheese, or Costa Rican Monte Rico cheese

Using a food processor or by hand, roughly chop the vegetables, somewhat fine, but not too much. When lopping off the tops of the bell peppers (with stems), save them for later. Separately, finely chop the herbs and set aside. Prepare the white rice according to directions on page 30.

In the iron skillet, take the ground beef and sauté in the olive oil over medium heat until cooked. Stir in onions, bell peppers, and garlic and sauté with beef two or three minutes until they begin to get tender. Turn heat down to the lowest it will go and stir in the slightly underdone white rice. Then stir in the tomatoes, and lastly add 1/2 of the herbs, salt and pepper and hot peppers.

Let skillet mixture simmer for 20 min. covered, on the lowest setting you have, occasionally stirring. Stir in other half of herbs. Taste for flavor and adjust. When ready to be served, lay the 2 slices of cheese on top, sprinkle paprika for color, and place the tops of the sweet pepper on top of that, so that stems poke out of the dish.

Serve hot in iron skillet to guests.

Arroz con Pollo

This is 'the' dish served at all large family gatherings and birthday parties in Costa Rica.

(Serves 5)

1 large, iron skillet
2 cups of slightly under-cooked rice
1 whole chicken breast, both sides,
    cubed
1 clove of garlic
1 cm of root ginger
1 leaf of basil (opt.)
1 tsp. of cilantro (opt.)
1 large carrot, cut julienne
1 large sweet bell pepper,
cut the same
1 medium-sized onion, sliced
1 stalk of celery, small, short slices
¼ cup of frozen sweet peas,
    thawed

2	TB of brown sugar	2	TB soy sauce
2	TB of peanut oil, or	2	TB of cooking sherry *(dry white)*
cooking oil (corn or sunflower)			

Heat the oil in the skillet as hot as can be without burning the oil. Do not use olive oil because olive oil has a low burning point. If you want the flavor of peanut oil, take peanuts and soak them in the oil. Throw in a little bit, but not all, of the garlic and ginger for about 30 sec. Sauté chicken until brown but not over cooked. Remove chicken from skillet and set aside. Turn heat down slightly. Put the rest of the garlic and ginger in and briefly sauté until you add all the vegetables. Cook for about 2 min. until just tender. Add brown sugar and sherry, add meat, then add the rice, tossing it like a salad with your spatula, making it cook even. When the rice looks like it has absorbed the oil and has a little color, turn heat off and let sit for about 5 min. Add the rest of the peanuts, toss a little and put into serving dish.

Picadillos

For something to be a picadillo, it needs to have some sort of starchy base like potatoes, boiled green plantains, pumpkin, or chayote and the usual Spanish dish vegetables and herbs of bell pepper, onion, garlic, cilantro etc. All must be finely cubed, English sauce to create cohesion, and flavored either with bits of ground beef or sausage.

Healthy and hearty, these go great wrapped in tortillas. Also great for leftover vegetables you might have. Feel free to improvise by adding some favorite or omitting a vegetable you don't have. Just make sure you maintain the basic principles mentioned above

Picadillo de Chayote

(Serves 6, can be stored in refrigerator)

1	**large iron skillet**
3	**light green chayotes**
4	**TB of ground beef or sausage**
1	**TB olive oil**
1/2 tsp.	**brown sugar**
1	**TB ketchup (for color)**
1/2 tsp.	**Salsa Inglesa** *(English sauce)*
1	**medium onion**
1/2	**large red bell pepper kernels of 1 medium size ear of sweet corn**
1	**small tomato, peeled**
1	**Scotch bonnet hot pepper**

By hand, carefully cube all vegetables. Sauté vegetable, except the tomato, in olive oil on medium low heat. Add ground beef (or sausage), then add the chayote.

The chayote will soften and shrink during cooking.

Now add your peeled tomato. At this point you can continue cooking with your skillet or throw the contents into a crock pot at low and cooked for about 3 hours. If you desire the skillet, continue cooking covered on med-low until the chayote is tender to taste. Stir in ketchup and sugar and salt and pepper to taste. Serve with white rice and tortillas.

Picadillo de Papas

(Serves 6, can be stored in refrigerator)

1 large iron skillet

3 medium potatoes, peeled
4 TB of ground beef or sausage

1 TB olive oil
1/2 tsp. brown sugar
1 TB ketchup (for color)
1/2 tsp. of Salsa Inglesa (English sauce)
1 medium onion
1/2 large red bell pepper
Kernels of 1 medium size ear of sweet corn

1 small tomato, peeled
1Scotch bonnet hot pepper
1   clove of garlic, minced
1   tsp Fresh cilantro
1   TB Fresh Spring onions

By hand, carefully cube all vegetables. Sauté all vegetables, except the tomato, in olive oil on medium low heat. Add ground beef (or sausage). The potatoes will soften and shrink during cooking. Now add your peeled tomato. At this point you can continue cooking with your skillet or throw the contents into a crock pot at low and cooked for about 3 hours.

If you desire the skillet, continue cooking covered on med-low until the potato is tender to taste. Stir in ketchup and sugar and salt and pepper to taste. Serve with white rice and tortillas.

Potato Arepas

(Serves 4)

1	medium skillet	2	TB of flour
3	TB of corn oil	2	TB of corn starch
3	cups of leftover mashed potatoes	1	small chopped onion
1	tsp. or less Salt	1	tsp. turmeric
1	beaten egg	¼	cup fennel seeds
			Chopped fennel
			Pinch of pepper

Mix the onion and spices to the refrigerated mashed potatoes (adjust salt as necessary, if salt has already been added), add egg, flour and corn starch. Mix thoroughly into a dough, adjust flour as necessary.

Heat a frying pan with oil and fry until browned on both sides.

Make into a loose ball and on hot skillet and after cooking for a while, flatten carefully with spatula. When brown, turn over and brown the other side.

Vinegar Salads and Pickling

These recipes come from my Indiana background. What is important are the ratios of vinegar, water, salt and sugar. The tastiest vinegar to use is apple cider vinegar. To pickle almost anything vegetable use this as your base:

½ **cup apple cider vinegar** *(never use white, distilled)*
2   **TB of sugar**
1   **tsp salt**
2   **tsp of olive oil**

Dissolve sugar and salt in the vinegar, and mix in the rest of the ingredients. For more briny mixture up salt to 1 tablespoon (TB), for more sweet, same amount of salt, double the sugar. Depending on your taste, some spice suggestions you may add:

1/8 to ¼ tsp of black pepper, or whole peppercorns
½   **tsp fennel seeds**
½   **tsp celery seed**
½   **tsp dry mustard**

Fennel (fresh, amount to taste)
Dill (fresh, amount to taste)
Oregano (fresh, amount to taste)
Thyme (fresh, amount to taste)

For your main vegetables (considering the amounts above) use:

3   **cups of shredded cabbage, either green or purple**
Or
5   **sliced or wedged cumbers**
Or
16 **ounces of string beans**
8 ounces of black bean
8 ounces of red kidney beans,
8 ounces of garbanzos

For your complimentary vegetables (considering the amounts above) use:

medium shredded Spanish onion
1 medium shredded carrot
1 stalk of celery, chopped
1 shredded hot pepper
1 medium sweet pepper

Select and prepare your main vegetables as directed. Then select and prepare the secondary ones. Combine with main vegetable. Prepare the vinegar base, combine, and lastly combine your preferred spices. Mix well.

Put into mason jars and refrigerate over night. Serve cold. Always refrigerate, wait at least a day, eat all before 2 weeks, and throw out remaining liquid in jar each time, don't reuse.

Breads

Sweet Breads

Sweet breads are really muffins in disguise. The difference is you put one in a loaf pan and the other in a muffin pan. Always with muffin recipes it is important to combine separately the dry ingredients and the wet ingredients. Then mix, but not never too much.

La Corona Cornbread

Dry ingredients:

1 cup all-purpose flour
¾ cup yellow cornmeal
½ cup sugar
1 tsp. salt
2 ½ tsp. baking powder

Wet ingredients:

1 beaten egg
1 cup milk
2 TB cooking oil (olive oil is preferred)

Extras:
½ cup sweet corn kernels
2 slices Monte Rico Cheese (Jack Cheese)

Preheat oven to 400°F. Grease a loaf pan or an 8 inch pan with center hole; set aside. Combine your dry ingredients in a medium mixing bowl. Make a well in the middle. Put egg in and beat it. Add milk and oil. Stir only until moistened and still lumpy. Carefully fold in corn and cheese.

Pour batter into pan, and bake at 400°F for 15 to 20 minutes.

Take out of the oven, and cool for at least 15 minutes. Take a knife to loosen the edges of the bread and turn over to take out of pan.

Banana Nut Bread

Dry ingredients:

2 cups all-purpose flour
1 ½ tsp. baking powder
½ tsp. baking soda
¼ tsp. ground cinnamon
¼ tsp. ground nutmeg

Wet ingredients:

2 beaten eggs
1½ cups mashed bananas (5 medium)
1 cup sugar
½ cup cooking oil (sunflower is preferred)

Extras:
½ cup chopped walnuts and/or almonds

Preheat oven to 350°F. Grease a loaf pan; set aside. Combine your dry ingredients in a medium mixing bowl. Set aside. Mix your wet ingredients in another bowl. Add the wet ingredients to the bowl of the dry ingredients all at once and stir only until moistened. Carefully fold in nuts and chocolates. Pour batter into loaf pan, and bake at 350°F for 50 to 55 minutes. When center is solid, take out of the oven, and cool for at least 15 minutes. Take a knife to loosen the edges of the bread and turn over to take out of pan.

Zucchini Chocolate Chip Bread

(1 loaf, 16 servings)

Dry ingredients:

2   cups all-purpose flour
1   tsp. ground cinnamon
½ tsp. baking soda
½ tsp. salt
¼ tsp. baking powder
¼ tsp. ground nutmeg

Wet ingredients:

1   beaten egg
1   cup sugar
1   cup finely shredded, unpeeled zucchini
¼ cup cooking oil (sunflower is preferred)
½ cup chopped walnuts and/or almonds
½ cup semi-sweet chocolate bits

Extras:

½ cup chopped walnuts and/or almonds
½ cup semi-sweet chocolate bits

Preheat oven to 350ºF. Grease a loaf pan; set aside. Combine your dry ingredients in a medium mixing bowl. Set aside. Mix your wet ingredients in another bowl. Add the wet ingredients to the bowl of the dry ingredients all at once and stir only until moistened. Carefully fold in nuts and chocolates. Pour batter into loaf pan, and bake at 350ºF for 50 to 55 minutes. When center is solid, take out of the oven, and cool for at least 15 minutes.

Take a knife to loosen the edges of the bread and turn over to take out of pan.

Ayote (Pumpkin) Bread

(2 loaves, 32 servings)

3 and 1/3 cups of all-purpose flour
2 tsps. baking soda
1½ tsp. salt
1 tsp. ground nutmeg
1 tsp. ground cinnamon
4 eggs
3 cups sugar
1 cup cooking oil (sunflower is preferred)
2/3 cups water
15-ounces of peeled and cooked ayote, or pumpkin (1 can or a quarter of the whole)

Extras:

½ cup chopped walnuts and/or almonds
½ cup raisins

Preheat oven to 400ºF. Sprinkle Ayote piece with salt underneath and roast until soft and the skin with easily come off with a fork (about 50 minutes). Remove from oven, let cool, take off peel and process in a food processor until smooth. Turn oven down to 350ºF. Grease 2 loaf pans; set aside.

In a big bowl (do not be tempted to do this by hand) beat the sugar and oil with an electric mixer on medium speed. Add eggs and beat well; set aside. In a smaller bowl combine the flour, spices, salt, and baking soda. Beating on low speed, alternately add the flour mixture and water to the sugar mixture. Beat in Ayote and fold in the extras. Pour batter into prepared loaf pans, and bake at 350ºF for 55 to 65 minutes. When center is solid, take out of the oven, and cool for at least 15 minutes.

Take a knife to loosen the edges of the bread and turn over to take out of pan.

La Corona de los Santos Pancakes (Arepas)

One last muffin recipe. People who don't like pancakes because they are too sweet usually like this recipe. Use with our fruit toppings or orange marmalade (page 46.)

(8 to 10 pancakes)

Dry ingredients:

1 cup all-purpose flour
2 TB cornmeal
1 TB sugar
½ tsp. baking soda
1 tsp. baking powder
¼ tsp. salt
¼ tsp. ground cinnamon
¼ tsp. ground nutmeg

Wet ingredients:

1 beaten egg
1 cup buttermilk, or whole milk
2 TB cooking oil (sunflower is preferred)
1 tsp. apple cider vinegar

Extras:

½ cup chopped strawberries or blueberries *(opt.)*

Heat griddle to where a drop of water "dances" when placed on it. Use about 3 TB of cooking oil. Turn down to medium low.

Combine your dry ingredients in a medium mixing bowl. Make a well in the middle. Put egg in and beat it. Add milk, vinegar and oil. Stir only until moistened and still lumpy.

Pour enough batter onto griddle to make a 13 cm circle. (Add individually fruit pieces as desired.) Wait until side starts to bubble and edges firm up. Take spatula and flip. Cook until centers are dry. (You will probably have to throw out the first one because it is too burnt or underdone.)

English Muffin Breakfast Bread

(2 loaves, 32 servings)

This muffin is really a yeast bread and if you've never made bread before this is a good starter and easy. Remember yeast is alive and needs a warm (not hot) temperature to rise. No kneading required!

6 cups all-purpose flour
2 pkgs. dry yeast
¼ tsp. baking soda
2 cups milk
½ cup water

1 TB sugar
1 tsp. salt

Preheat oven to 400ºF. Grease loaf pans, about 2 TB of cornmeal inside each pan and roll around until inside of pans are coated; set aside.

Mix 3 cups of flour, the dry yeast, and baking soda well in a big mixing bowl. In a medium saucepan combine sugar, salt, milk and water. Warm up liquid to "a little too hot to touch" (130ºF). Add to flour mixture, combine well with a wooden spoon.

Mix the rest of the flour until you have a lumpy dough. Divide equally in half and put one part in one pan and another in the other. Wet a clean dish towel and place in the sun for about 45 min. to double in size.

Put into the center of the 400º heated oven and bake for about 25 min. or until golden brown.

A portal to the heavens: the terrace fountain.

Photo: James N Holland

The garden gate.

Photo: Roy Gamboa

Desserts
And Sweets

From the Caribbean!

Castle Black

Rum Cake

I had tasted this dessert in many Jamaican restaurants and had enjoyed it with many friends from the Lesser Antilles. Finally it was a good friend from Trinidad that provided me with traditional instructions to make this delicious – and sinful! - cake.

(Serves about 15 people, can be stored indefinitely by adding Rum to moisten)

1 large baking pan

½ lb. butter (unsalted)
½ lb. sugar
¾ lb. flour
5 eggs
1 tsp. baking soda
1 tsp. of ground whole clove
1 tsp. of whole allspice
1 tsp. of cinnamon
Add nutmeg to taste (about 1 teaspoon)

½ lb. EACH of dried prunes (seedless), raisins, currants
¼ lb. EACH of dried red cherries, dried mixed tropical fruits
        (pineapple, guava, mango, papaya), *(opt. shredded coconut)*
¼ lb. almonds (coarsely chopped)
1 pint browning, about 3 small bottles. *(Find in the international isle of the supermarket / Jamaican. You can also just burn sugar to make the browning you need.)*
1½ cup cherry brandy
Favorite rum to taste
1 tsp. vanilla extract

Pre-Preparation:
Preheat oven to 300? F.
Butter or spray non-stick oil into a cake mold to bake in.
Leave butter out for at least 30 min.

Pre-Preparation:
Cream butter. sugar and vanilla until light and fluffy.
Add eggs one at a time, then add all dry ingredients.
Fold in dried fruits with a spatula
Add browning / cherry brandy into cake batter.

Pre-Preparation:
Bake cake at 300?F for 3 hours or until when poked with a toothpick, the toothpick comes out clean. Let cake cool thoroughly, then on wax paper or a serving plate, flip the mold upside-down and let cake loosen and fall to plate. Thoroughly soak with poured rum, cake will keep indefinitely. If dried out, add more rum before serving. Serve with whipped cream or ice cream.

Bread and Cream

(Serves 1)

One thick slice of any of the sweetbreads (see p. 37 -40)

1 scoop vanilla ice cream   **Whipped cream**
1 TB Coffee Liqueur   **Cinnamon or Nutmeg**

The hardest part is of this is making the sweetbread. Cut the slice in half, put in a dessert bowl, pour the coffee liqueur over the bread, place the scoop of ice cream, next the whipped cream and sprinkle with cinnamon or nutmeg.

Quick Castle Sugar Cookies

(Serves 10)

1 cup of sugar   **¼ tsp. Baking soda**
¾ cup of vegetable shortening   **1 tsp. Cinnamon**
1 egg   **1 tsp. Vanilla**
¾ tsp. Cream of Tartar   **2 cups of flour**
1 tsp. Baking powder   **2 TB of yellow cornmeal**

Heat oven to 375º. Stir until you have a cream the sugar and vegetable shortening. Add egg and vanilla. Mix very well. On top add flour and cornmeal, then baking powder, cream of tartar, cinnamon, and baking soda. Mix dry ingredients on top, then mix well into the cream below. Make into spoon-sized balls and place Evenly on the a baking sheet. Bake for 11-15 min. In center of oven. Take out and let cool on a rack for at least 30 minutes.

Arroz con Leche

(Serves 8)

1 cups cooked rice
4 cups water
1 cinnamon stick
4 cloves
Zest of Lime
2 whole eggs
3 cups whole milk
18 oz. can of sweetened condensed milk
Deseeded Guayabitas or Raisins
1 tsp. of vanilla
(Opt.: 1 oz. Whiskey)

In a large saucepan combine rice, water cinnamon stick, cloves and lime zest. Let sit covered for 1 hour. Then bring the mixture to a boil and turn down the heat to medium. Cook until almost all the water is evaporated. About 10 minutes.

In a separate bowl mix well the eggs with the whole milk, then add the sweetened condensed milk, vanilla (and whiskey). When the rice mixture is ready add the milk mixture. Add the raisins. While constantly stirring, adjust the heat as necessary, first bringing the mixture to a slight boil and then lowering the heat to medium and stir until thickened, about 25 minutes.

When desired consistency is reached. Let cool for 1 hour. Serve warm or cold. Pudding will thicken even further with time, so do not overcook.

Fruit Toppings ("Miel")

Whether it be mango, oranges, pineapples, apples, peaches, or strawberries. Use this recipe for a quick fruit topping. The trick is cornstarch, the same ingredient that is used to thicken puddings and many Asian sauces.

1 medium saucepan
3 cups of chosen fruit, peeled, de-seeded and chopped *(p. 6)* **or
    favorite tropical fruit**
1 cup sugar
3 TB of cold water
2- 3 TB corn starch

In the saucepan add the fruit and sugar. In a small cup combine the corn starch and water to combine until you have a liquid. Stir into the mixture in the pan and heat until bubbling, constantly stirring. Let bubble for about 2 minutes or until you've reached your desired thickness.

7 cup (250 ml) jars
    *(either bought or recycled from clean,
    used jarred goods from the supermarket)*
1 large sauce pot
1 liter of chuck-chopped orange pulp
    *(about 10 medium, take out seeds
    and center rinds)*
**2 cups of thinly sliced orange peel from
    the oranges**
1 cup thinly sliced and seeded lemon
    (about 2 medium)
2- 4 TB of corn starch

Real marmalade will not be like the hard, jelly kind you buy in the supermarket. Marmalades will have more "motion." I'll tell you later how to get the consistency you prefer later in the recipe.

For now, combine all ingredients, except the sugar in the pot. Simmer for about 5 minutes and then cover and let it sit for about an afternoon and night. In the morning, measure what you have, measure a cup of sugar for every cup of this orange pulp "stew." Put the pot back on the stove and on high heat, letting the peel tenderize (about 10 min. when boiling). Now add the sugar, stirring constantly, and boil the heck out of it until the water steams out. It will become sticky and start to gel.

(Now, here's the trick, for assured thickness, dissolve about 2 to 4 tablespoons of cornstarch in a 1/4 cup cold water. Add it to the boiling pot.)

Now remove from the heat, stirring every once in while to prevent sticking. While hot, ladle this syrup into your jars, place on covers. To "can" these and create a vacuum, half-submerse tightly capped jars in boiling water for about 10 minutes. Remove. As they cool, they should "pop," which basically means they are sealed.

Drinks

Coffee

"Coffee" and the *"Los Santos Valley"* are interchangeable words. Whether is be from the canton of León Cortés, Tarrazu, or Dota, this region produces the best coffee in the world purchased by some of the crowned heads of Europe.

Coffee is a fruit that was discovered in Ethiopia and made into a beverage by the Arabs from the roasted seeds. The type of coffee we drink is called *"Arabica."*It was brought to Costa Rica in 1750. And today Costa Rica produces only 2% of the world's coffee, but it is considered the highest quality.

For the most flavor, it is best to store whole beans in a vacuum-tight container and in a dark, cool place. **Never put your coffee beans in the freezer or refrigerator to store!** This will destroy the oils inside the beans which give coffee its taste.

There is more information in our *"La Corona de los Santos Coffee Tour Book"* which can give you the history of roasts and drink recipes. But for starters, here is a recipe that is one of my favorites and puts a little spin on the flavor.

"Smoked" coffee
2 ½ tsp. of coffee to every cup of water
1 tsp. of lightly roasted sesame seeds
1 tsp. of yellow corn meal

Fruit Drinks ("Frescos")

Also known as "smoothies", these simple drinks made out of fresh fruit are very healthy alternatives to soda. Even diabetics can enjoy them by substituting sweetener. Here in the mountains we have many fruits to choose from; *guayabita, tokoka, guava, cas, níspero.* (p. 6) To keep the juices a little longer, after straining them, bring the juice to boiling (*níspero* is necessary to bring to a quick boil), let cool to room temperature and then refrigerate.

Raspberry (or "*Mora*") Fresco
2 cups of Raspberries
2 TB of sugar or 1 TB of sweetener
4 cups cold water
4 ice cubes

Put all ingredients in a strong blender that crushes ice. Blend thoroughly until there are no chunks left. When finished, pour through a strainer in a pitcher or directly into your glass.

Agua Dulce

(Makes 4-5 servings)

½ cake of Dulce or adjust to desired sweetness
4 cups water
1 cup milk

In a medium to large saucepan boil the water. Add the Dulce, stir until dissolved. Take off heat and add the milk. Serve in coffee cups.

The coffee fields of Santa Cruz de León Cortés.

Photo: James N Holland

Index

*** Denotes Authentic Costa Rican recipe!**

Made in the USA
San Bernardino, CA
10 December 2019